Happy Bi

JOSEMARIA ESCRIVA

by
Helena Scott & Ethel Tolansky

All booklets are published thanks to the generous support of the members of the Catholic Truth Society

CATHOLIC TRUTH SOCIETY
PUBLISHERS TO THE HOLY SEE

CONTENTS

Beginnings

A Friend in Madrid

It was a blazing hot morning in Madrid in 1930. A young priest who had been to visit a sick friend was walking home, since he could not afford to take a bus. For no particular reason he took a different way from his usual one. Suddenly he heard his name, "Josemaria!" He looked up. "Isidoro! How wonderful to see you!"

"I've just been looking for you," exclaimed Isidoro. "When I found you weren't at home I was going to find a restaurant to have lunch, and then catch my train. I'm going up north; my family are already there for the summer. It's odd, but I had the strangest feeling that I'd meet you if I turned down this particular street."

The meeting was providential for both of them. Isidoro Zorzano was working as a railway engineer in Malaga, in the south of Spain. "I feel unsettled," he said. "I believe God is asking something of me, that I've got to 'do something'. But I don't really know what it could be. I thought that maybe God was calling me to join some religious order, but I can't see that clearly. I've got my job as an engineer, and I'm perfectly happy with it. I don't know what to think. I need some guidance from you."

Father Josemaria Escriva looked at his friend in astonishment. "Do you remember my letter?" he said. "Well, it was precisely because I wanted to talk to you about a new undertaking I've started."

Father Escriva had moved to Madrid from Saragossa three years previously, in order to study for a doctorate in civil law. While there, God had shown him what he had been praying and searching for ever since he was a teenager. He now knew that God wanted him to help ordinary people to find God in their daily lives, becoming saints in and through their everyday work or study. But until now, it had been difficult to find people who could understand fully what this entailed, and commit themselves to working alongside him. He had written to Isidoro earlier that year, "When you come to Madrid, don't fail to look me up. I have some interesting things to tell you." Now Isidoro's words made it plain that he was looking for something very like the way of serving God that Father Escriva was setting up.

Father Escriva hesitated, realising that if Isidoro accepted the call, he would be committing himself for life to an undertaking he had only just been introduced to. Father Escriva needed time to think and pray about whether this was really the right decision for Isidoro to make, so at his suggestion they separated for lunch and met again later on that day. Meanwhile, he prayed for light. He could see that on the one hand Isidoro could not move to Madrid, so he would have to learn about this new path to God at a distance; on the other hand, the fact of meeting in the street at a time when each needed the other, was clearly providential. After careful prayer and reflection, Father Escriva made up his mind.

When they met again in the afternoon he began to describe to Isidoro, in broad strokes, the panorama of sanctifying work in everyday life - in his case, the work of a railway engineer. As he listened, Isidoro realised that his place of work could become a meeting-place with Christ, his job a path leading him directly to holiness. His desire to give himself to God and his professional vocation were no longer in conflict. He could give himself completely to God by doing his work responsibly and well, and making it into something holy.

"I can see the hand of God in this coincidence," said Isidoro enthusiastically. "You can count on me. As far as I'm concerned, my mind's made up." From that day on, for the rest of his life, he considered himself committed to God our Lord to serve him in this Work of God - in Latin "Opus Dei".

Early life

Josemaria Escriva was born in northern Spain in 1902. He was the second child in the family. His parents, Jose and Dolores, were comfortably off though not rich, and had four daughters as well as Josemaria: Carmen, who was three years older than him, and Asuncion, Dolores and Rosario after him. When he was two he fell so seriously ill that his life hung by a thread. His parents begged our Lady to intercede for him, offering him to her if he could be cured, and he recovered quite suddenly. To show their gratitude to our Lady, they took him on a pilgrimage to the ancient shrine of our Lady of Torreciudad, high in the Pyrenees.

Both his parents were committed and practising Catholics, with a fervent devotion to the Blessed Sacrament, and they had the custom of saying the Rosary as a family at home. To the end of his life, he remembered the prayers his mother taught him to say almost as soon as he could talk. When he was six or seven, he made his first Confession, and when he was ten, his First Communion.

However, tragedy soon struck the happy family in earnest. Those were times of high infant mortality, and Rosario, the youngest of the family, died when she was just nine months old, in 1910. In 1912 Dolores died at the age of five, and the following year Asuncion, aged eight, also died. She had been ill for a little while, and when Josemaria went in one day to ask his mother how she was, Mrs Escriva answered bravely, "She's quite well now - she's in Heaven." She found the strength to comfort him and helped him to see that people belonged to God, and God took them to Heaven because he wanted them to be happy with him. Later on, thinking about his three little sisters, Josemaria, then aged eleven, started saying that it would be his turn to die next, because he was the next in age. His mother reminded him, very simply, of how our Lady had saved his life already when he was a baby, and how he had been specially offered to her, so that she was sure to protect him. Realising that this was true, and also that he was causing his mother additional suffering, Josemaria soon stopped repeating the idea.

When Josemaria was twelve Mr Escriva's business failed. The fault was not his, but he insisted on paying off all the creditors himself, which left him bankrupt. The family left their home town of Barbastro and moved to Logroño, not far off, where Mr Escriva took a job in a clothing store. From then on money was very tight, and Josemaria learnt from his parents how to be cheerful and not complain when there was not enough of something to go round.

He went to the state school in Logroño. He was a bright, hard-working boy with a good sense of humour and a great gift for making friends. It was here that he had first met Isidoro Zorzano.

Footprints in the snow

Six months before he left school, at the age of sixteen, something happened which had a profound effect on him. One snowy morning Josemaria went out early, and saw on the ground something which brought him to a standstill. It was a line of footprints in the snow, left by a Carmelite friar who had just passed that way barefooted. On seeing the sacrifice offered by this holy man, Josemaria felt the Holy Spirit stirring his heart, and making him ask himself what sacrifices *he* was prepared to make out of love for God.

Up until that time, he had thought of training to be an architect, since he had an aptitude for drawing and mathematics. Now, however, he felt the need to place himself entirely at God's disposal, and he took the decision to do so by becoming a priest, something he had never even considered before. To begin with, he increased his acts of devotion, going to daily Mass and Communion to seek union with Jesus Christ, and frequent Confession to get rid of any obstacles there might be to the Holy Spirit's dwelling in his soul.

He went to talk over his desires to serve God with the Carmelite friar whose footprints he had seen in the snow. The friar suggested that he could enter Carmel himself. Josemaria felt quite clear that God was not calling him to become a religious, but had other plans for him, although he did not yet know what they were. By this time, however, he was sure that they included the priesthood.

He also, in due course, talked to his father about it. For the first time in his life, he saw Mr Escriva shed tears. He said, "My son, think it over carefully. A priest has to be a saint. It's very hard to have no home and no love on earth... Think about it a little more, but I won't stand in your way." Josemaria took his father's words into account, and furthermore, he realised something his father had left unsaid - that his decision would involve his parents and sister in additional hardship, since they had been looking to him to take over the support of the family from his father in due course. He decided to pray for his parents to have another son. He always felt it was in answer to his prayers that a year later his brother Santiago was born.

On his father's advice, Josemaria went to talk to two priests who were well known for their holiness and wisdom. However, the future they could see for him failed to match up with his notion of putting himself entirely at God's disposal. They explained that after working in a country parish for some years he could progress steadily through the administrative system of the Church to become a canon, a member of the diocesan curia, director of the diocesan seminary, and so on. Josemaria felt sure that he did not have a vocation to be a religious, but he also felt that a successful career in the hierarchy was not what God had in mind for him either.

Call to the priesthood

In spite of this, he remained convinced that God was calling him to be a priest, and he had the courage to go ahead with no clear idea of where he might end up. In September of the same year, 1918, he started attending the Logroño seminary as a day-student. After two years he transferred to the Pontifical University in Saragossa, living as a boarder in the seminary of San Francisco de Paula. During the whole of this time of training for the priesthood, he constantly repeated phrases from the Old and New Testaments which he used as prayers and aspirations: "Lord, that I may see!" *(Mark 10:51)*; "Lord, what do you want me to do?", like St Paul on the road to Damascus *(Acts 22:10)*; "Here I am, because you called me!" *(I Samuel 3:9)*. He begged to be able to see God's plans for him in their fullness, so that he could carry them out.

Then and throughout his life, he turned to the Gospel account of our Lord's life to nourish his prayer and inspire his actions. He loved to contemplate the different scenes in the Gospel by taking part in them as one of the characters there. As we have just seen, he found he could use many of the Gospel phrases as short vocal prayers to help him keep in God's presence throughout the day.

He got on well with his fellow-seminarians, although because of their very different backgrounds, there were times of difficulty and conflict which served to form and strengthen his character. They remembered him afterwards as an excellent student with a warm personality, a ready sense of humour and very high standards of personal and social behaviour. He spent a lot of time praying in front of the Blessed Sacrament to see what God wanted from him as a priest.

At the same time as completing his studies for the priesthood, Josemaria, on his father's advice, began studying for a law degree at the University of Saragossa. In Spain at that time, when there were very many vocations to the priesthood, it was not impossible for priests to train for a profession not directly connected with the Church, as long as it was compatible with the priestly ministry. Josemaria was never afraid to take on more than one thing at a time. He continued his law studies until he got his degree, but he always made sure that they did not take time away from his theological studies or, later, his work as a priest.

Ordained a priest

His courage and generosity in setting out to follow God's will did not mean that his path was free from difficulties or sorrow. His father died quite suddenly at the age of fifty-seven, in November 1924, three weeks before Josemaria was ordained a deacon. Early in the next year his mother brought Carmen and Santiago to live in Saragossa, not far from the seminary, since all of them now depended on Josemaria for support. On 28th March 1925, Josemaria was ordained a priest. His love for the Mass, always a central part of his inner life, took on a new dimension now that it was his voice and his own anointed hands that brought Jesus to the altar.

Three days later he was sent to a country village called Perdiguera to take the place of the parish priest, who had been taken ill. He worked there for the next seven weeks, celebrating Mass, hearing Confessions, taking Holy Communion to the sick, and teaching catechism to children.

This short period was to have a lasting effect on his life. He came face to face with the extreme poverty of the peasants and the hard, lonely life of the country priest, seeing at first hand how much the country people needed help. It was the beginning of a heartfelt concern for diocesan priests, shown in his loyal friendship to those he knew personally, and his readiness to do whatever he could to help his fellow-priests all over the world, in all sorts of ways. His experience in Perdiguera was one of the things that led, many years later, to the setting up of rural schools and agricultural training centres around the world, under his inspiration, to help country people in their working lives, while taking care of their cultural and spiritual needs as well.

Further Studies

On 18th May Father Escriva returned to Saragossa and took up his law studies again. While devoting his time to his priestly ministry and his studies, he continued to pray intensely for light to see the whole of God's will for him.

As at every period of his life until the day he died, he took care of his relationship with God by centering it on his daily Mass, and by setting himself small, specific points of struggle on aspects where he saw that he needed to improve. At the end of each day he examined his conscience to see where he had offended God or missed a chance of loving him more. He always started his examination of conscience by making an act of humility in God's presence, and finished with a sincere act of contrition, making a resolution for the following day's fight. He never gave up the struggle against his faults or weaknesses. As he once expressed it, "These are the ripe fruits of a mortified soul: tolerance and understanding for the defects of others; intolerance for one's own" (*The Way*, 198). When he realised that he had failed in a point of struggle, instead of being discouraged and giving up, he was always ready to begin trying again, as often as necessary.

He passed his law exams in 1927, supporting his mother, sister and brother by teaching law at a private academy. He asked his Bishop for permission to transfer to Madrid in order to take his doctorate in civil law at the university there, and was granted permission to move to Madrid for two years.

Caring for the sick

In Madrid, as well as continuing his law studies, he worked as chaplain for a charitable institution run by nuns called the Foundation for the Sick. This work brought him in contact with the very poorest people in the city slums. He taught catechism to children, prepared them to make their first Confession and First Holy Communion, and visited the sick in hospitals and in their homes. He spent many hours a day walking from one part of Madrid to another, and was always ready to be called upon by the nuns no matter what was involved or how tired he was. He often went to look after the terminally ill in the overcrowded hospitals for the poor, where people suffering from tuberculosis stayed until they died, since in those days no treatment for it had been discovered. Isolated from their families for fear of contagion, the patients were in a wretched state, lonely, in pain, and afraid. Father Escriva brought them help and comfort with his tremendous faith and warmth, teaching them to see God's loving hand in all that happened to them. When he ministered to the sick, he asked them to pray and offer up their sufferings for a special intention of his. This intention was that the "something" which God was asking of him would become a reality.

He was not always well received by the people he went to visit. Anti-religious feeling was gathering strength in those times, and sometimes, as he went through the slum districts in his cassock, people would shout abuse and throw stones at him; or he would call at a house and have the door slammed in his face. He was not discouraged or frightened off, but prayed for all these people to find the truth.

Founding Opus Dei

On 2nd October 1928 Father Escriva was praying alone in his room after Mass, during a retreat. He was going over some notes he had made of the series of inspirations and lights which God had been granting him over the past years. As always, he prayed for light to see God's will more clearly, feeling that there was something very specific God wanted of him, but that he had not yet grasped what it was. Suddenly, as he afterwards described it, he "saw" exactly what it was that God was asking him to do. His sense of blind searching was replaced by a clear, distinct image or message in his soul. The thing that he had been praying for, and getting others to pray for, without knowing what it was, had become clear at last. He had found his full vocation; he knew what path he had to follow. Although it did not yet have a name, Opus Dei was born at that moment.

Holiness in daily work

Everything in his life up till that time fell suddenly, dramatically into place. He understood how all Christians were called by God to be real, canonisable saints by the fact of their Baptism. And he saw a multitude of ordinary, everyday Christians who would dedicate themselves to reaching holiness and union with God in their daily work by doing it well and offering it wholeheartedly to God. Since holiness meant genuine identification with Christ, it would be outward-looking and expansive: as close followers of Christ, they would help those around them to seek Christ, to find him in their own work, and fall in love with him too, turning that work into prayer. Because it would be done by ordinary people working in every different kind of job, from shoe-repairing to astronomy and from lecturing to ship-building, this apostolate would have no limits - it would be, as he put it later, like a shoreless sea.

Father Escriva could see that his own task was to teach people *how* to find God in their work. The ideal that now filled him was something virtually unheard-of in the early part of the twentieth century. Nearly forty years later, the Second Vatican Council was to spell it out in detail in the Dogmatic Constitution on the Church (*Lumen Gentium*), "The laity, by their very vocation, seek the kingdom of God by engaging in temporal affairs and by ordering them according to the plan of God. They live in the world, that is, in each and in all of the secular professions and occupations. They live in the ordinary circumstances of family and social life, from which the web of their existence is woven. They are called there by God so that by exercising their proper function and being led by the spirit of the Gospel, they can work for the sanctification of the world from within, in the manner of leaven" (no.

31). "All the faithful of Christ, of whatever rank or status, are called to the fullness of the Christian life and to the perfection of charity" (no. 40).

The mission of lay people

As Father Escriva said later, work is the hinge on which the holiness of lay-people turns. His whole message could be summed up in the triple phrase, "Sanctify yourself in your work, sanctify your work, and sanctify others through your work." He talked about "passionately loving the world", because it was created by God, has been redeemed by him, and needs to be brought back to him. This involves both rights and duties, because people who are trying to find God in the world need to take full responsibility in civil society. A key concept for him was "secularity", meaning that lay-people took responsibility for their own actions and actively tried to find ways of doing apostolate themselves, in union with and obedience to the Church and its hierarchy. It meant that, just as the clergy should give the lead to other members of the Church in the liturgy and the Sacraments, and the religious through the practice of the evangelical counsels, lay-people should give the lead in offering the world to God by finding out in practice how to sanctify the world of business, economics, manufacturing, the service industry, teaching, research and development, and all the other spheres where they live and work. To

Father Escriva secularity also meant love for freedom, and universality: he never excluded anyone from his respect and prayers, because, as he said, "each soul is worth all the Blood of Christ".

Put your heart into what you are doing

He helped people to see that, to sanctify the work they do, they need to try and practise all the virtues in it - both the supernatural virtues of faith and hope and love for God and for those around them, and the "human" virtues, as he called them, such as tidiness, order, punctuality, loyalty, professionalism, cheerfulness and constancy. He was to write, "Do you really want to be a saint? Carry out the little duty of each moment: do what you ought, and put your heart into what you are doing" (*The Way*, 815). He often underlined the immense value of little things, and finishing things off down to the very last detail. Work done lovingly in this way becomes prayer, real communication with God.

Work is normally where people meet, and is therefore a very important place for Christian apostolate. Father Escriva always stressed that a good example has to come first, because people would be inclined to listen to those who really practised what they preached, and who had good standing because they worked hard and well.

Father Escriva knew that spreading these new ideas would be something that demanded not only all his own energy and commitment, but that of many other dedicated people too. For some time he did not think of it in terms of an organisation with a title; in his own mind, and when he spoke of it to others, it was simply "what God is asking of me", "the apostolic task", or "the work of apostolate". But one day in early 1930 the priest to whom he used to go to Confession asked him, "And how is that work of God coming on?" Father Escriva was struck by the appropriateness of the phrase as a name for his undertaking. "The Work of God", or in Latin "*Opus Dei*": surely that expressed exactly what he was trying to do. From then on, he adopted it as the name of the enterprise, often shortening it simply to "the Work".

Opus Dei takes shape

Externally, his life continued as before. Opus Dei grew and took shape slowly and silently within his soul, while he continued his care of the poor and sick, as well as preparing his doctoral thesis, and again teaching Roman Law and Canon Law at a private academy to support his family.

Father Escriva visited many seriously ill and dying patients in the Madrid hospitals for the poor. He went not only as a priest, taking them the Sacraments and helping them to offer up all their sufferings to God, but also to do for them many of the practical things they could not do for themselves - washing them, cutting their nails, brushing their hair, and even emptying the bed-pans. He did it very cheerfully and lovingly. As he was soon to say in a book he was putting together at the time, "Everything done for the sake of Love acquires greatness and beauty" (*The Way*, 429). Even when these tasks made him feel sick, he never showed it, but always made the patients feel loved, and not forgotten or abandoned. He helped them to see what he was convinced of himself: that their sickness was a treasure, if they united their sufferings to those of Christ on the Cross, and could be a power-house of grace for the whole Church. He himself relied on the help of their prayers for the grace to establish the Work and its apostolates.

On Sunday afternoons he invited young men whom he had met through his apostolate to go to the hospitals with him and join him in his work there, and he taught them to do it with the same loving care for the sick. These visits to the very poorest patients in hospitals made a deep impression on the young men, since they could see at first hand the contrast between their own lives and the lives of the people they were caring for; and also, how God's love could be present in the midst of all kinds of suffering.

Father Escriva was helped for a while by another zealous young priest called Father Jose Maria Somoano, until Father Somoano died suddenly in July 1932, in all probability having been poisoned by an anticlerical fanatic. Father Escriva remembered him with gratitude for the rest of his life. In the same year Luis Gordon, one of the first laymen to join him in Opus Dei also died, and ten months later the first woman who had committed herself to Opus Dei, called Maria Ignacia Garcia, died of tuberculosis. She had joined Opus Dei when she was already ill, and offered up all her intense sufferings for the future apostolate of Opus Dei. Many other patients in the hospitals contributed the offering of their illnesses for the same intention, and to Father Escriva this was true riches.

God as Father

It was in 1931, when Father Escriva was going through some particularly difficult times, that he had received a very special gift from God - a totally new awareness of what it means for Christians to have God for their father. He was on a tram in Madrid one day when he suddenly felt the reality of his divine sonship in its fullness, and for some time he was so absorbed in the discovery that all he could do was repeat "*Abba, Pater!*", the Aramaic and Latin words for "father" which are found in the Gospel, when Jesus was praying to his Father God in his agony in the garden, and which St Paul takes up in his letter to the Galatians, *(4:4-6)* "Because you are sons, God has sent the Spirit of his Son into our hearts, crying 'Abba! Father!'"

From that time on, the sense of being a son of God was the basis of Father Escriva's whole spiritual life, and something he passed on to the people of Opus Dei as fundamental. Like every Christian, he knew that Christ is the only-begotten Son of God, and those who are united to Christ through baptism become God's adopted children, but what they do with this adoption depends on their own free use of God's gift. Now Father Escriva understood that sufferings of every description could become a way not only of sharing in Christ's Cross, but of being so closely united to Christ as to become one with him. He loved Christ so much that sharing in Christ's sufferings was a source of real joy to him, and he used a characteristic phrase of his own to express the paradox: "our happiness has Cross-shaped roots". Being one with Christ also meant having an absolute, child-like trust in God's fatherly care, in big things and in small ones. He wrote, "Each day, O my God, I am less sure of myself and more sure of you!" (*The Way*, 729).

For the rest of that year (and, indeed, for the rest of his life) he spent a lot of his periods of prayer on developing and deepening this sense of being a "very small" child of God. In December, one morning after Mass, Father Escriva's love for Jesus and our Lady overflowed into a booklet called "*Holy Rosary*", which he wrote there and then. It was a commentary on each of the mysteries of the Rosary as seen through the eyes of a loving child, watching and taking part in them as they unfolded. When the booklet was published Father Escriva was happy to feel that it helped people to get to know Jesus and our Lady better through her Rosary.

Learning about apostolate

Father Escriva gave spiritual direction to a growing number of young men. Some of them felt the call to dedicate their lives to God in Opus Dei, and said yes to it. Father Escriva spent a lot of time with them, often walking through the Madrid streets or gathering in a small café much frequented by students. He ensured that they thoroughly understood the meaning of seeking holiness in the world, and started them along the paths of the interior life, showing them how to keep in contact with God at every moment of their day, whether they were studying, working, travelling, relaxing at home or with friends, or talking to God in a loving personal conversation. He taught them to make an examination of conscience every day on specific points, as he did himself, and to make resolutions to fight on for the following day. He also took them to his mother's flat, where they learnt from the Escrivas the family atmosphere that was so characteristic of Opus Dei. And he taught them how to bring their friends into contact with God in their turn. Years later, he said in a homily which was afterwards published, "Apostolate is love for God that overflows and communicates itself to others. The interior life implies a growth in union with Christ, in the bread and in the word. And apostolate is the precise and necessary outward manifestation of interior life. When one tastes the love of God, one feels burdened with the weight of souls... For a Christian, apostolate is something instinctive. It is not something added on to his daily activities and his professional work from the outside. I have repeated it constantly, since the day that our Lord chose for the foundation of Opus Dei! We have to sanctify our ordinary work, we have to sanctify others through [it]" (*Christ is Passing By*, 122).

Role of women

In 1930 Father Escriva had understood, as a result of a further inspiration from God, that women too were to be included in Opus Dei - so far he had only been thinking in terms of men. He began to speak about the spirit of the Work to some of the young women who came to him for Confession and spiritual direction. He was clear from the start that the men and women in the Work would be completely independent of and separate from each other in every aspect of their lives and apostolate. Accordingly, he never included women in the projects and activities he was organising for young men, and to begin with, his apostolate with women went much more slowly. Although he was naturally impatient to see Opus Dei develop, he refused to force things, certain that if he did all he could, and backed it up with a lot of prayer and mortification, God would bring the Work along at his own pace. Many of the first young women who came in contact with the Work were introduced to Father Escriva by their brothers or cousins, who were already friends of his. Among those who came to understand the spirit of the Work were Lola Fisac, Encarnacion Ortega and Nisa Gonzalez. They were later to help spread the Work to new countries, including England.

In spite of being only a few years older than the people who joined the Work, Father Escriva was like a real father to them. Not only did he care for their spiritual lives, living his priesthood to the full, but he loved them deeply and was concerned about everything that happened to them. When Isidoro Zorzano joined the Work in 1930 he naturally addressed Father Escriva on equal terms, as an old friend. Very soon, however, he came to see Father Escriva as a father, speaking and writing to him with the confidence, affection and respect of a son. He adopted the habit of addressing Father Escriva as "Father", not only because he was a priest but to express what all the people of the Work were to feel: Father Escriva was truly their father in the spiritual life, and Opus Dei was a real family. Before long, they all called him "Father" and referred to him as "the Father" when they spoke of him.

The first Centre of Opus Dei

The early 1930s were a period of violent hostility to religion in Spain, and many Catholics' minds turned to politics as a way of resisting the growing forces of atheism and anarchy. Father Escriva, while respecting everyone's individual choice, always made it clear that he had nothing to say about politics, because as a priest his role was to bring Christ to everyone. One of the best ways he could think of to fulfil this aim was to provide places where young people could learn to study and work seriously, and at the same time learn about the Catholic faith by seeing it lived out in daily life. In December 1933 he set up the "DYA Academy", which was a rented flat where students could go for extra tuition in certain subjects, or simply to study in a congenial atmosphere. Although he had very little money, he worked hard and with the help of the few young men who had joined Opus Dei by that time, made sure that the surroundings were as welcoming and home-like as possible, and also that everyone who came to the "Academy" realised that study was something to be taken very seriously in itself, and which, when done well and conscientiously, could be offered to God. As he said, "An hour of study, for a modern apostle, is an hour of prayer" (*The Way*, 335).

He had so many demands on his time that it seemed impossible to get through the day, and yet he never lost sight of his need to put his relationship with God first. If, on looking at the day ahead, he saw that it was going to be difficult to do his prayer, for example, at the time he normally set aside for it, he always tried to bring it forward rather than putting it off. On getting up in the morning, he often still felt tired from the day before, and he would sometimes promise himself, "I'll have a rest before lunch" as an encouragement to keep going. But when he saw the huge amount of work awaiting him, he would say, "Josemaria, I've fooled you again!" He knew there would be no chance of a rest.

The Apostolate Grows

'The Way' is published

In the middle of all this hard work he was gathering a series of points for prayer and reflection based on his own experience. He soon had enough to publish them in book form, and in 1934 the first edition of *The Way* came out, under the title "*Spiritual Considerations*". It was written in such a way that all sorts of people could use it to guide their prayer and discover God's presence in their daily lives. It consisted of short paragraphs, usually addressed either to the reader or to God, collected in chapters around various themes - the Holy Mass, prayer, work, mortification, apostolate, interior life, our Lady, little things, and many more. It made an excellent introduction to the spirit of Opus Dei, showing how ordinary people could keep up their relationship with God and do apostolate in all the various circumstances of their lives. Directed especially towards young people, it contained very practical suggestions and pointers for forming the character ("Get used to saying No," 5), and for tackling all sorts of situations in daily life with a Christian outlook. "Many great things depend - don't forget it - on whether you and I live our lives as God wants" (755), is one comment, and another says simply,

"A little act, done for love, is worth so much!" (814). The thread running through the whole book is love for God, expressed in deeds and overflowing to other people: "Lord, may I have balance and measure in everything - except in Love" (427).

Meanwhile the first flat Father Escriva rented for the DYA Academy had become too small for all the activities taking place there. In autumn 1934 he transferred it to a larger one, and offered not only teaching and study facilities but also accommodation for a small number of university students. Father Escriva did a fair amount of the housework himself, helped by a number of young men who had come to understand Opus Dei and committed themselves to it. From the start, Father Escriva gave them a full share in the work and apostolate. However, he always made sure that they realised that their work and apostolate had to be the result of a living relationship with God in prayer. In this way he avoided the danger of their falling into "activism" - undertaking a lot of good projects while neglecting the effort to deepen their relationship with God, fight against their defects, and make progress in the virtues.

One of those who joined the Work at this early stage was a young engineering student called Alvaro del Portillo. He quickly understood and absorbed the spirit of Opus Dei, and was to become a lifelong help and support to Father Escriva, who relied on him as on a rock.

Help with new ventures

During all this time, Isidoro Zorzano had been working in Malaga, in the south of Spain, coming up to Madrid to see Father Escriva whenever he could. He put his heart into learning about the spirit of Opus Dei and applying it to his own life day by day, and with Father Escriva's help he steadily built up a solid relationship with our Lord, centred on his Real Presence in the Blessed Sacrament. By determined efforts, Isidoro learnt to offer every part of his work to God, to spend a fixed time in daily prayer and meditation, to examine his conscience every day and set himself aims in his spiritual struggle, and to treat his students, and the people who were working for him, with unfailing fairness, kindness and consideration.

In addition to his visits to Madrid, which were necessarily infrequent, he wrote to Father Escriva regularly in order to keep up with the progress Opus Dei was making, as well as asking for advice on his own spiritual life. When he heard of the efforts everyone was making to set up the new students' residence and make a success of it, Isidoro did not hesitate, but with characteristic generosity sent some of his own pay to Father Escriva, for him to use however he thought best. Father Escriva appreciated this help, since most of the people who had joined the Work so far were still students, and were not in a position to give financial help, though they were all prepared to work hard themselves to do whatever was needed. But renting the two flats for the residence and Academy, and equipping them with furniture and fittings, necessarily cost money. Father Escriva's mother and his sister, seeing the difficulties he was faced with, generously decided to sell off some property which they had recently inherited, and used the proceeds to buy what was needed.

It was not rashness that made Father Escriva start something he had not enough money to do. He acted out of faith. He knew God wanted this new path of complete dedication in the middle of the world to be opened to many people; he felt it was urgent; and he was convinced that if he did all that he possibly could, God would not let him down. He saw himself as an instrument that God could use for the good of souls if he was faithful, and he trusted God completely.

Like the flat he had originally rented, the apartments occupied by the students' residence became too small for all the activities being carried on there, and with the other people of the Work, Father Escriva managed to find a larger place, planning to move there at the end of the academic year, July 1936. In June of that year Isidoro had finally left his job in Malaga and moved to Madrid, where he could help with the Father's projects. Since there were now several people in Opus Dei who had been well formed in its spirit and ideals, Father Escriva was planning to send some of them to live in Valencia and other cities in Spain, and then Paris, to continue the apostolate among young people and workers there. Isidoro was to take charge of the Madrid students' residence, and he threw himself wholeheartedly into the task, quickly familiarising himself with every detail of the work there, and helping with the move to the larger apartment. However, all these plans were abruptly cut short by the outbreak of the Spanish Civil War, on 18th July 1936.

War in Spain

Spain was divided in two. The Republican side was loyal to the Popular Front Government, and was on the whole violently anti-Catholic. Their ranks included significant numbers of anarchists who wished to do away with all constitutional rule, and communists. The other side was called the Nationalist side. It was in general loyal to the Catholic Church and wished to restore it to its former position, which had been undermined by successive laws over the previous years. The situation had reached the point where the two sides were unable to negotiate at all, and the result was civil war. Most of the Army had risen in revolt against the Government in support of the Nationalist side.

Madrid was firmly in the Republican zone, and, as a priest, Father Escriva's life was in danger. Militia groups were stopping people in the streets and demanding their identity papers at gun-point; any priests or religious were usually either shot or hanged on the spot, and so were countless other people simply for being practising Catholics. On the day of the Army uprising itself, Father Escriva had to leave the new students' residence disguised in workmen's overalls, and he could not go back there again because sooner or later the militia would come to look for him. Nor could he stay with his mother, for fear of putting her life in danger too. He spent nearly three months going from one place to another in Madrid, never staying anywhere for long, and in constant danger.

Constant danger

On one occasion he was in a flat with several other refugees, one of whom, Juan Sainz, did not know he was a priest. Militiamen suddenly arrived and started to search the whole building systematically, working from the basement upwards, to find any priests or other "suspicious" characters. Father Escriva and those with him climbed up into the attic. They heard the search drawing close and knew that they would probably be killed if they were found. Father Escriva did not want those with him to die without at least receiving absolution, and so he said in a whisper, "I'm a priest. This looks bad. If you wish, make an act of contrition and I'll give you absolution." As Juan said later, "It was a big risk for him to tell me he was a priest. To save my own life I could have turned him in." Other people's souls literally mattered more to Father Escriva than his own life. The searchers, however, missed the attic they were hiding in.

At another point he showed similar courage to defend his own vocation. One of the people in the Work, a brilliant but rather absent-minded man, came to meet him one day in triumph, announcing that he had found a flat where Father Escriva could live in security. He handed him the keys. It seemed like a miracle - a safe haven, instead of having to dodge from one hiding-place to another. On questioning him, however, Father Escriva learnt that the flat was looked after by a woman in her twenties. He refused to expose his vocation as a priest to the danger of living at close quarters with a young woman, and to put himself out of temptation, he dropped the keys down a drain in the street.

Throughout all this time he stayed calm and cheerful, maintaining his faith that everything and everyone was in God's hands. Some of the people in Opus Dei had left Madrid before the Civil War broke out to spend the summer with their families in other parts of Spain, and although they were also in the Republican zone, at least the danger for them was not so immediate, and Father Escriva could be relatively easy on their account. Those of his spiritual sons in Opus Dei who were still in Madrid were his constant concern. Some had gone into hiding; some had been drafted into the Republican army; and some had been imprisoned.

Isidoro spent two months without leaving his mother's house, since he was being hunted by some communists from Malaga who knew that he was a fervent Catholic and that he had moved to Madrid. At the end of the two months, however, the hunt had been abandoned and, moreover, his appearance had changed considerably - he was much thinner, had a different haircut, and was wearing tinted glasses. He felt it was possible to move around the city, especially since he had a paper certifying that he had been born in Argentina. Although he did not actually have Argentinean nationality at that stage, the paper was enough to protect him in spot searches by militia patrols. He was of enormous help to Father Escriva, since he used his relative freedom of movement to find and visit the other people of Opus Dei and keep them all in touch with one another.

Safe haven in Madrid

At one stage Father Escriva took refuge in a most unlikely hiding-place - a lunatic asylum. The doctor in charge of the asylum offered protection to a few people who were in danger of being killed, concealing them among his real patients. Father Escriva was even able to celebrate Mass there a few times, which he had been unable to do while on the run. The hiding-place was not ideal, but he stayed there until in March 1937 he was able to move to a slightly safer place, the Honduran Legation in Madrid, which was also offering protection to those in danger of death for being on the wrong side. There, Father

Escriva was joined by four other people of the Work, and his younger brother, Santiago, who was now eighteen. He was able to celebrate Mass almost every day thanks to Isidoro, who managed, with difficulty, to provide altar-breads and wine. The six of them shared a very small room. Living conditions were very cramped, the food which the Legation was able to provide for the refugees whom they were sheltering was extremely poor, they were unable to leave the building, and their stay there could have been a nightmare. Instead, Father Escriva showed them how to use the difficult circumstances to develop their relationship with God and their respect, concern and affection for other people. He took special care to see that they used their time well, spending a certain amount of time each day praying, studying foreign languages, writing letters, and keeping the room clean and tidy. He helped them realise that although they were practically prisoners, it could be a time of inner growth instead of a time of idleness which would leave them slack and despondent. As a result, their stay in the Honduran Legation was something which they always looked back on afterwards as a very special episode in their lives.

Moving on

At the end of five or six months Father Escriva took the decision to leave the Honduran Legation and try to find a way of getting over to the part of Spain controlled by the Nationalist side, so that, free from religious persecution, he could continue the apostolate that God had given him to do. He was driven by the urgency of this task even in the terrible circumstances of a civil war. It was, however, a very hard decision to take, since it would mean leaving his mother and sister, and some of the people of Opus Dei, in Madrid. He trusted God absolutely, convinced that if they were all determined to do God's will, whatever happened to them would be ultimately for the best.

When he left the Honduran Legation he had with him some papers attesting that he was an employee of the Honduran Legation and so had diplomatic immunity. It was over a month before he could leave Madrid, and he lived meanwhile much as he had at the start of the war, moving constantly from one place to another. He used this time to celebrate Mass in different people's houses, take the Blessed Sacrament to other people in hiding, hear Confessions, and even preach a spiritual retreat for five people. Those attending the retreat would meet in one place for a conference, then disperse and meet somewhere else for the next one, to avoid being noticed.

Escape from Madrid

Finally, with a small group of other people of the Work and friends, he made his way to Barcelona, and from there they escaped from the Republican zone of Spain on foot over the Pyrenees Mountains. It was a very harsh, dangerous journey, in which all their lives were constantly threatened both by the difficult conditions and by the border guards, who would shoot suspected fugitives on sight. With a number of other refugees, they were guided through the difficult mountain tracks by a series of smugglers, who undertook the job for money, and at one stage their guide threatened to abandon one of Father Escriva's companions called Tomas Alvira, who was so exhausted he was unable to keep up with the rest. Father Escriva, however, refused to allow this. He took the man aside and reasoned and argued with him until he changed his mind and they all continued together, supporting Tomas as best they could between them.

In spite of the difficulties of the journey and the very rough terrain, at one point - a Sunday - Father Escriva made an opportunity to celebrate Mass. The Catholics in the group gathered as near him as possible, and one of them wrote later in his diary,

"The most moving moment of the trip was the holy Mass: a priest in our company said Mass on a rock. He didn't say it like the priests in the churches. His clear and heartfelt words penetrated to our souls. I've never heard Mass like today. I don't know whether it's because of the circumstances or because the celebrant is a saint. Communion was moving. We could barely move, we were dressed in rags, dirty and unshaven, our hair needed combing, our bodies needed sleep, our hands were bloodied with scratches, our eyes shone with tears; above all, God was with us in the host."

Others who heard Mass said by Father Escriva, at every stage in his life, confirmed that he put his heart and soul into every word of it.

After two gruelling weeks they arrived in Andorra, and crossed back into the Nationalist zone of Spain via France. They went to Burgos, where Father Escriva, although extremely thin and weakened by all that he had been through, at once plunged into the task of recommencing his apostolic work.

For the next sixteen months he worked intensely. He wrote letters to all the people of the Work he could locate, and many friends, using a kind of coded language to evade censorship when he was writing to Isidoro and others in the Republican zone. He wrote and duplicated newsletters as well, to keep the people of Opus Dei and their friends up to date with each others' activities. He preached spiritual retreats. He travelled endlessly, visiting his spiritual sons in Opus Dei wherever they were, to give them spiritual guidance and more material, fatherly help as well. Whenever they were able to obtain leave, they came to see him in Burgos. They always went away with some clear guidelines on maintaining their relationship with God and doing apostolate in their present circumstances.

Beginning again

The Spanish Civil War was over by the beginning of April 1939, and Father Escriva had already returned to Madrid on 28th March. He went to the building where they had started the new Academy so hopefully nearly three years before, and found it had been so heavily bombed that nothing remained except a few of the walls. Instead of being discouraged, he and the other people of the Work set to work again from scratch, with energy and optimism, and six months later a new hall of residence and centre of Opus Dei opened its doors in Madrid. Very shortly afterwards another centre was opened in Valencia.

Retreats and spiritual direction

Father Escriva was beginning to be much in demand among Bishops all over Spain, and at their request travelled from one city to another giving retreats to priests of different dioceses, and to groups of religious and lay-people. He put his heart into giving them as well as he could, keenly aware of how important it was for priests in particular to be holy and close to God. Throughout his life, giving retreats to priests, and preaching or giving spiritual direction to them, made him feel very humble, because he saw them as outdoing him in virtues and dedication.

The next seven years were a period of both hardship and growth for Opus Dei in Spain. Father Escriva still dedicated a lot of his time to working with sick and destitute people in Madrid hospitals. By now he was also giving spiritual direction on a regular basis to a great many men and women of all ages, from all sorts of backgrounds. He spent long uncomfortable hours in third-class carriages of trains travelling to different parts of Spain, to give retreats and conferences not only to priests but to groups of students and working people. He encouraged them to deepen in their knowledge of the Christian faith, to value the Sacraments, to find and follow Christ through hard work in their ordinary everyday lives, and to help bring those around them to God.

Dolores and Carmen Escriva

As well as all this he was very much involved in setting up and running the centres in Madrid and other cities which were the focal point for much of the apostolate done by his sons in Opus Dei. In this he was helped enormously by his mother, Dolores, and his sister Carmen. They undertook the cooking and housework in one centre after another, and through it succeeded in making them into real family homes, cheerful and welcoming places. This took their combined skill, energy and considerable ingenuity, since the people of Opus Dei had very little income between them, and in any case it was a time of great scarcity in Spain. To the aftermath of the Civil War were added the effects of the Second World War which was now raging in the rest of Europe, making supplies of every kind very hard to come by.

The year 1941 brought an unexpected blow: in April, Father Escriva's mother died after a short illness. He was away giving a retreat to priests in another city, and so did not even have the consolation of being with her in her last

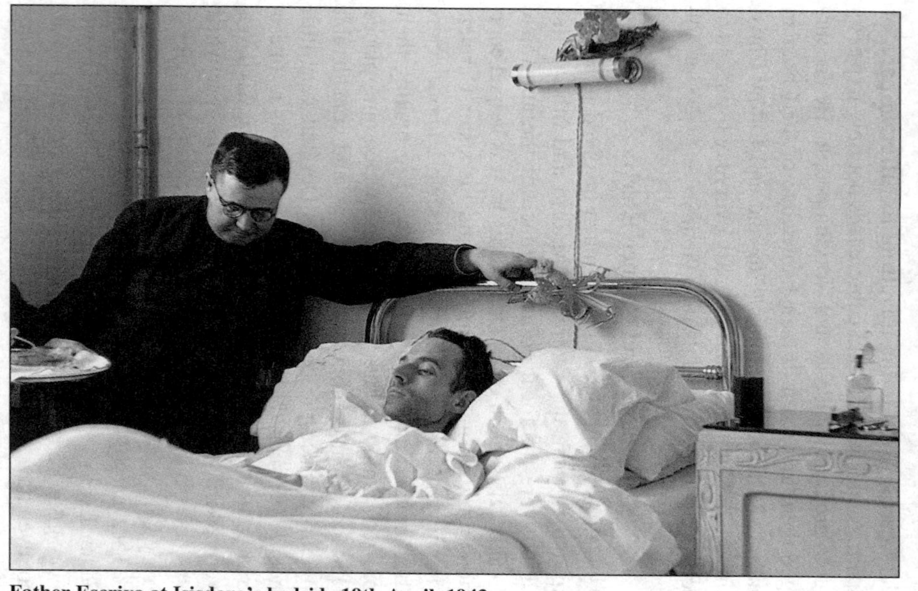

Father Escriva at Isisdoro's bedside 19th April, 1943.

moments or giving her the Sacraments. He suffered very much over this, but offered it up for the apostolate with priests, which he always saw as being of great value to the whole Church. After their mother's death, Carmen carried on looking after the domestic work, helped in due course by the women who joined Opus Dei. She taught them all she knew, which was by now a great deal, about the practicalities of cooking, laundrywork, and housekeeping on a slim budget.

Isidoro

As if the loss of his mother were not enough, Isidoro Zorzano, who had been working at his side since the end of the Spanish Civil War, and had been an immense support to Father Escriva, fell ill of Hodgkin's Disease in the same year, and after gradually getting worse, died on 15 July 1943. Throughout his illness Father Escriva and the other people of the Work had given him all the care and affection they could. He never at any stage complained of his sufferings, which towards the end of his life were intense, but offered them and his life itself to our Lord for the Father and the apostolates of the Work. The process for his beatification was opened in October 1948.

Road to Evangelization

Priests in Opus Dei

As the number of people who received a vocation to Opus Dei grew, they helped Father Escriva in his apostolate, and in teaching those who had joined Opus Dei more recently about the spirit of the Work. The part of his apostolate they could not help him with, however, was hearing Confessions. Not only was this a fundamental part of all apostolate with Catholics, but frequent Confession and spiritual direction was also essential to the spiritual life of everyone in Opus Dei. It was becoming clear that Opus Dei would need to have priests ordained from among the people who already belonged to it, since they would be able to guide others in the spirit of the Work because they were practising it themselves. What was not clear was how this could be done, since normally priests are ordained either to serve the diocese they come from or to serve the religious order to which they belong, and Opus Dei was neither a religious order nor a diocese.

After much searching, Father Escriva received the answer to the problem while he was celebrating Mass on 14th February 1943. The Priestly Society of the Holy Cross was set up as an integral part of Opus Dei, and

Alvaro del Portillo and two other people of the Work who had duly completed their studies for the priesthood were ordained priests on 25th June 1944. They were to be the first of many. For Father Escriva this was a further development of his aim of service to the Church - Opus Dei was providing lay-people with a path to holiness in ordinary life, and was also contributing priests to the Church, to serve all souls.

At the same time, in accordance with Father Escriva's vision of what Opus Dei should be like, priests did not form a separate group or class within the apostolate of Opus Dei, but priests and lay-people did their apostolate in organic unity. As Pope John Paul II was to say many years later, addressing people of the Work on 17th March 2001, "It will be the direct witness of lay people (...) that will reveal how it is only in Christ that the highest human values attain their fullness. (...) Priests, on their part, perform an irreplaceable primary function: that of helping souls, one by one, by means of the Sacraments, preaching and spiritual guidance, to open up to the gift of grace. A spirituality of communion, therefore, will enable the role of each one of these constitutive ecclesial elements to be appreciated to the full."

Opus Dei attacked

By 1946, people of the Work had opened centres in eight cities in Spain as well as one in Portugal. While Opus Dei was developing in these ways, Father Escriva also had to face a growing amount of opposition to his work. Some Catholics at the time saw the clergy as being the essence of the Church, and thought that the only thing lay-people could do was try to lead good lives, join in the apostolate organised by the clergy, and, if they wished to aim for perfection, either become religious or at least imitate a religious rule of life as much as they could. They tended to think that daily work in the world and ordinary social life were necessarily obstacles to holiness. Such people did not consider that laymen and women could aim for true holiness in their everyday, working, married lives. When Father Escriva preached precisely that, these people decided it must be a new kind of heresy.

Misunderstood

Furthermore, Opus Dei was not aligned with any political group, and so could not claim the support they might have offered. Father Escriva upheld the personal freedom of each of the people in the Work to choose their own way in political matters, opting for the solutions that seemed best to them, and he never referred to politics except to say that they were not his business, since he was a priest and was concerned with people and their souls, not political parties. But his message of universality and freedom was not always understood by people outside the Work. As well as being denounced as a heretic, he was also accused of leading young people astray and even of forming an undercover political movement himself. Father Escriva, with the help and support of the Bishop of Madrid, worked long and patiently to overcome these misunderstandings.

Consolidating and expanding the Work

Once the long war years, first in Spain and then in the rest of Europe, were over, Father Escriva felt that the time had come to spread the message of Opus Dei to other countries. In order for Opus Dei to take root abroad and develop as it should, it would need to be officially recognised by the Church at a universal level, not just in Spain. This meant obtaining approval from Rome, the seat of the universal Church. So in June 1946 Father Escriva moved to Rome himself, and settled in a very small flat, with a handful of other people of the Work, in order to get Opus Dei properly established within the framework of the Church.

The flat they rented was very close to the Vatican, and from one window they could see the windows of the Pope's apartments. Father Escriva had enormous devotion to the Holy Father as Christ's representative, the visible head of the Church. He was so deeply moved by being so close to him that, tired as he was after his long journey, on his arrival he stayed up for the whole of his first night in the flat, in a vigil of prayer for the Pope.

Father Escriva with Pope Paul VI at the Centro ELIS, Rome, November 21, 1965.

His loyalty to the Holy Father was not limited to praying for him. All along the different stages in the development of the Work, Father Escriva took advice from the Church hierarchy and requested approval for each new step. This was especially true when the time came to draw up the statutes for the government of the Work. This was the result of his concept of Opus Dei as existing solely to serve the Church, something he often underlined.

The Church officially approved the character and development of Opus Dei in stages, and Father Escriva worked patiently to ensure that the task would be fully achieved. This was not something he found easy, because he was quick and impulsive by nature, and he had to curb his natural impatience to get things done. What was more, he felt a sense of urgency to bring the message of Opus Dei to as many people as he could. The long delays involved in getting all the canonical steps duly completed were a great trial for him, and demanded a lot of fortitude and supernatural outlook on his part.

In all of this Alvaro del Portillo was a tower of strength. Father Escriva had sent him to Rome to speak to the Holy Father and the Roman Curia about Opus Dei even before he moved there himself. Now a priest, "Don Alvaro", as he was always called, was constantly at Father Escriva's side. He was a man of outstanding intelligence and ability, but never sought the limelight, devoting all his talent and energies to providing Father Escriva with faithful, loyal friendship, help and support.

Family life

From the start of the Work, Father Escriva had seen it not only as something demanding full-time dedication from single people, but also as a call to married people who could live out its spirit in their family life. From 1948 onwards the first married people joined the Work. Father Escriva helped them to see how to "do Opus Dei" in the context of their families, stressing the vital importance of friendship between children and parents. He emphasised that marriage is a divine vocation and a path to holiness, and that married people are called to be contemplatives, to be saints and to do apostolate, in and through their married life. Family life, he taught, involved spending time together, taking care of one another, listening, learning each other's likes and dislikes, and being the first to forgive. He also taught them that if it is to be genuine, married love must be open to receiving children from God; he said that love that "blocks the sources of life", as he put it, is really only selfishness. Married people have the help of a special Sacrament with its sacramental grace, to fulfil their calling.

Those who receive a specific vocation from God to dedicate their lives to him, owe 90% of that vocation to their parents for the upbringing they have provided, according to Father Escriva. He made sure that the people of the Work never neglected their responsibilities to their parents and families, and that they always kept in touch with them even when the needs of the apostolate or other circumstances separated them. Towards the end of 1941 he asked one of the young men in the Work, whose parents had had to go into exile in Algeria at the end of the Spanish Civil War, "How long is it since you last wrote to your parents?" "Perhaps a month and a half now, Father," replied the young man. Father Escriva told him firmly that he should not have left them so long without a letter, since in their situation one of their few pleasures would be getting letters from their son. And he added, "Go and write them a letter ten pages long, on both sides, straight away."

Apostolate with diocesan priests

He had always had a great affection and concern for diocesan priests, and came to realise that the call to seek holiness through one's daily work which was the essence of Opus Dei, could be a vocation for diocesan priests just as much as anyone else, since their priestly, pastoral ministry is the daily work which they are called to sanctify and in which they can find God. Those priests who heard and responded to this new vocation would find that it strengthened their primary vocation to the priesthood and involved no conflict of loyalties: Opus Dei provided spiritual training and support, enabling them to appreciate all the more fully the value of close unity with their Bishop. Father Escriva spent a lot of time with diocesan priests who came to see him in Rome or when he was on his travels.

Father Escriva had a tremendously broad vision. His view of the activities of the Work included people from all walks of life, people of other Christian denominations and people who belonged to other faiths or none. Many of these were attracted by his message and found that without actually joining the Work themselves, they too had a role to play in it. They became firm friends and cooperators of the Work throughout the world.

Working in new countries

He began the expansion of the Work in earnest, and sent people of the Work to set up centres in most of the countries in Western Europe, including Italy, Portugal, England and Ireland; in North, Central and South America; and later in Kenya, Japan, Australia, the Philippines and Nigeria. He sent them with very little money, since he had none himself and they would need to support themselves, like anyone else, through their work, but gave them his blessing and a statue of our Lady. He always followed their development closely, and, while giving them full responsibility and freedom, supported them unfailingly with encouragement, advice and prayers. Sometimes Father Escriva took the initiative in sending people of the Work to start their apostolate in new countries; and at other times, he responded to invitations from

Bishops around the world to set up the activities of the Work in their dioceses.

Prayer and daily work

He was able to pass on his breadth of vision to his spiritual sons and daughters, so that they shared his own concern to improve the conditions of life in the countries they went to. Like him, they were not deterred by the fact that they had to start off in a very small way. Of greatest importance, as always, was their ow n relationship with God, through their prayer and daily work. Then, before any large-scale projects, came their personal apostolate, done through their work and based on friendship and good example. With Father Escriva's encouragement and guidance, they brought a Christian viewpoint to bear on the problems of poverty, unemployment, and lack of education which they found. In due course, and with the help of many other people, they set up all sorts of social and educational projects to help people whom many would classify simply as "disadvantaged", but whom Father Escriva saw as possessing the dignity of God's children. These projects, although very different from one another, all focused on enabling people to realise that all Christians, as such, are called by God to holiness, and that this holiness is to be found in the faithful fulfilment of daily duties and responsibilities in their working lives.

One project which he was able to follow closely was the Centro Elis, which was a technical training school in the slum district of Rome to enable manual workers to acquire skills and qualifications. In Mexico, people of the Work, with help from many others, developed a huge, derelict estate called Montefalco into a rural training centre, where peasants, mostly Mexican Indians, trained in agricultural skills and also in domestic skills and child-care. All of this was unheard-of in that area and was badly needed. In Peru, a similar project was set up called Cañete. He insisted that the college that people of the Work and their friends started in Kenya had to be inter-racial, although this was well before Kenyan independence and, as a total innovation in the country, aroused a fair amount of opposition. Father Escriva encouraged his spiritual children to tackle the difficulties they encountered with the courage born of knowing they were doing God's will; as he had put it in *The Way* (*733*), "Trust always in your God. He does not lose battles" and, "Jesus, whatever you *want*, I *love*!" (*773*).

The Way of the Cross

His courage in facing suffering himself, and his ability to help other people to see it and undergo it in a supernatural spirit, was the result of his deep love for our Lord's Passion and Cross. From the very beginning of his priestly ministry he often gave people books on the Passion to read, so that by meditating on what Christ suffered for mankind, they could learn to love him better and follow in his footsteps. In the early 1960s he wrote a commentary on the Stations of the Cross to help people of the Work to practise this devotion. After his death this commentary was published, with the addition of a number of passages from his other writings, under the title *The Way of the Cross*.

Travels

Not content with sending help and encouragement from Rome, Monsignor Escriva, as he was by now, spent much of the last part of his life travelling to different countries, accompanied as always by Don Alvaro, to see his sons and daughters in the Work and meet the people who were attracted to their apostolate. He spent the summers of five successive years, from 1958 to 1962, in England, partly to be able to work intensely in rather cooler temperatures than those of Rome in August. However, he did not allow the pressure of his work to prevent him from meeting as many of his spiritual sons and daughters, and cooperators and friends, as he could. He told them how much he appreciated the multi-cultural atmosphere of London, and that it was a "crossroads of the world" which should spur them on to do a fruitful apostolate with people of all the different nationalities to be found there. He also remarked on some fine examples of architecture and design he had seen as he visited different parts of the city.

A further reason for his journeys was his love for the Church. Many of them took the form of penitential pil-

Father Escriva at a meeting in Altoclaro, Venezuela, 10 February, 1975.

grimages, often centred around shrines of our Lady, to ask God's forgiveness for sins, and pray for the needs of the Church. Thousands of people came to listen to him and meet him, in large or small groups or individually, and he spoke to them about the basic truths of the faith, as he had done all his life, explaining the value of work, people's need for the Sacraments and especially the Sacrament of Reconciliation, the meaning of marriage and family life, and the responsibility of Catholics to spread the faith and help one another to practise it. He spoke out passionately in defence of the Church, and was not afraid to talk about the Cross, sacrifice and mortification.

A subject he was never tired of talking about was sincerity. He would say that first of all, people need to be sincere with themselves, in their personal examination of conscience, to acknowledge what they have done wrong and why. He underlined the importance of being sincere in their conversation with God, so as to make prayer into a genuine, heart-to-heart conversation with our Lord and not a formal, anonymous discourse. Then they need to be completely sincere in Confession and spiritual guidance, having the courage to talk clearly about the things they have done wrong without concealing anything, making excuses, or justifying themselves. This is the only real basis for sincerity and truthfulness in one's whole life and relationships with others. In all of this he was laying bare his own approach to the interior life, and advising others to do what he had found invaluable himself.

Although some of these gatherings were attended by huge crowds of people, his warm personality and, still more, his obvious love for God and for them as individuals made everyone there feel as if it was just a friendly, personal conversation. In the questions and answers which were exchanged, people could feel his constant good humour. This was always one of his most notable characteristics, and sprang from his awareness of being in the presence of his father God. He gave himself tirelessly to others during these journeys just as he did at home, and his encouragement and appreciation were a great help to the apostolate being done by his spiritual sons and daughters in the Work, with their friends and cooperators, in the countries he went to.

After an intensely busy two-week visit to Central and South America in February 1975, Monsignor Escriva returned to Rome and resumed his normal daily routine of hard work. This included seeing people who came to visit him from all over the world, and talking to them about their own concerns, encouraging them to centre their lives on Christ in all their different circumstances. He made a point of drawing them closer to our Lady, teaching them to treat her as "the Mother of God and our Mother too", and he spoke and wrote about her as often as he could. He also spoke constantly about loving, supporting and obeying the Pope.

In the task of governing and directing Opus Dei he had enlisted the help of a council made up of senior people of the Work, including Alvaro del Portillo. From the very beginnings of the Work he established that all of its management had to be collegiate, meaning that decisions on the organisation and development of the Work and its apostolates were never taken by one person alone - not even Father Escriva himself - but in consultation and agreement, after matters had been duly studied.

The death of Fr Escriva

On 26th June 1975, on a working day like all the rest, he died suddenly in Rome of a heart attack. Those with him saw that his last conscious act was to give a loving look at a picture of our Lady of Guadalupe, which was in his office.

He was seventy-three when he died. Although some parts of his life read like an adventure story, most of it was so quiet and simple that it could seem dull to anyone who did not grasp its depth. His life was his message, and his message was the importance of putting love into everyday life, into the ordinary things that very often go unnoticed except by God. As he wrote in *The Way* (817), "*Great* holiness consists in carrying out the *little* duties of each moment." The centenary of his birth, 9 January 2002, is a reminder that ordinary Christians in every century are loved by God and specially called to love him with all their hearts in return.

Josemaria Escriva was beatified by Pope John Paul II on 17th May 1992, at a ceremony attended by about 300,000 people from many different countries.

Bibliography

Josemaria Escriva, *The Way*, Scepter, London, 1987 (many other editions).

Josemaria Escriva, *Holy Rosary*, Scepter Publishers, Chicago, 1972 (many other editions).

Josemaria Escriva, *Christ is Passing By*, Veritas Publications, Dublin 1974.

Josemaria Escriva, *The Way of the Cross*, Scepter, 1982.

Peter Berglar, *Opus Dei: Life and Work of its Founder Josemaria Escriva*, Scepter, London, 1994.

Salvador Bernal, *Msgr. Josemaria Escriva de Balaguer: a profile of the founder of Opus Dei*, Scepter, 1977.

Francois Gondrand, *At God's Pace*, Scepter, 1989.

Dennis Helming, *Footprints in the Snow*, Sinag-tala/Scepter, 1986.

Jose Miguel Pero-Sanz, *Isidoro Zorzano*, Ediciones Palabra, Madrid, 1966.

Andres Vazquez de Prada, *The Founder of Opus Dei: the life of Josemaria Escriva de Balaguer (Vol. I)*, Scepter Publishers, Princeton, NJ, 2001.

Second Vatican Council, Dogmatic Constitution on the Church *(Lumen Gentium)*, in *The Documents of Vatican II*, Geoffrey Chapman, London, 1972. CTS Do 349.